Divine Mercy Prayer Book

"I trust in Your Mercy!"

by
The Marian Fathers

*All booklets are published thanks to the
generous support of the members of the
Catholic Truth Society*

CATHOLIC TRUTH SOCIETY
PUBLISHERS TO THE HOLY SEE

The Marian Fathers
Divine Mercy Apostolate

Contents

Dedication

Souls who spread the honour of My mercy I shield through their entire lives as a tender mother her infant, and at the hour of death I will not be a Judge for them, but the Merciful Saviour. At that last hour, a soul has nothing with which to defend itself except My mercy. Happy is the soul that during its lifetime immersed itself in the Fountain of Mercy, because justice will have no hold on it. (*Diary*, 1075)

Introduction

The purpose of this Prayer book is to help you to discover the depth and richness of God's Mercy. The mystery of God who is rich in Mercy was fully manifested in Jesus Christ.

By the revelation given to the Polish nun, St Sister Maria Faustina Kowalska, (25th August 1905 - 5th October 1938) we are called to trust in God's Mercy, and to share and exercise it in daily life.

The years St Faustina spent at the convent of Sisters of Our Lady of Mercy were filled with extraordinary gifts, such as revelations, visions, hidden stigmata, participation in the Passion of the Lord, the gift of bilocation, the reading of human souls, the gift of prophecy, and the rare gift of mystical engagement and marriage. The living relationship with God, the Blessed Mother, the angels, the saints, the souls in Purgatory - with the entire supernatural world - was as equally real for her as was the world she perceived with her senses. In spite of being so richly endowed with extraordinary graces, St Faustina knew that they do not in fact constitute sanctity. In her *Diary* written on advice of her spiritual director - Blessed Fr Michael Sopocko, she wrote:

> Neither graces, nor revelations, nor raptures, nor gifts granted to a soul make it perfect, but rather the intimate

union of the soul with God. These gifts are merely ornaments of the soul, but constitute neither its essence nor its perfection. My sanctity and perfection consist in the close union of my will with the will of God. (1107)

The message of the Divine Marcy is nothing new, just a reminder of what the Church has always taught: that God is merciful and forgiving and that we, too, must show mercy and forgiveness.

But, in the Divine Mercy devotion, the message takes on a powerful new focus, calling people to a deeper understanding that God's love is unlimited and available to everyone - especially the greatest sinners. As Jesus said to St Faustina:

The greater the sinner, the greater the right he has to My mercy (723).

Devotion to the Divine Mercy involves a total commitment to God as Mercy. It is a decision to accept His mercy with thanksgiving, to trust completely in Him, and to be merciful as He is merciful. The devotional practices proposed in the *Diary of St Faustina* and set forth in this Prayer Book are completely in accordance with the teaching of the Church and are firmly rooted in the Gospel message of our Merciful Saviour. Properly understood and implemented, they will help us grow as genuine followers of Christ.

There are two scriptural verses that we should keep in mind as we engage in these devotional practices:

1. "This people honours me with their lips, but their hearts are far from me" (*Is* 29:13);

2. "Blessed are the merciful, for they shall obtain mercy" (*Mt* 5:7).

Which of these would you like to hear the Lord say about you? It's an ironic and somewhat frightening fact that many of the most religious people of Christ's time (people who were actively practicing their religion and eagerly awaiting the promised Messiah) were not able to recognise Him when He came.

The Pharisees, to whom Christ was speaking in the first quotation above, were very devoted to the prayers, rules, and rituals of their religion; but over the years, these outer observances had become so important in themselves that their real meaning had been lost. The Pharisees performed all the prescribed sacrifices, said all the right prayers, fasted regularly, and talked a lot about God, but none of it had touched their hearts. As a result, they had no real relationship with God, they were not living the way He wanted them to live, and they were not prepared for the coming of Jesus.

When we look at the Image of the Merciful Saviour, or pause for prayer at three o'clock, or pray the Chaplet - are these things drawing us closer to the real sacramental life of the Church and allowing Jesus to transform our hearts?

Or have they just become religious habits? In our daily lives are we growing more and more as people of mercy? Or are we just giving "lip service" to God's mercy?

Asking for the Lord's mercy, trusting in His mercy, and sincerely trying to live His mercy in our lives, we can be assured that we will never hear Him say of us, "Their hearts are far from Me," but rather that wonderful promise, "Blessed are the merciful, for they shall obtain mercy."

It is our hope that you will make the prayers, attitudes, and practices presented in this Prayer Book a real part of your life. May you come to trust completely in God and live each day immersed in His merciful love - thus fulfilling the Lord's command to let your light "shine before people, so that they will see the good things you do and praise your Father in heaven" (*Mt* 5:16).

Most of the prayers and meditations in this prayer book are based on the texts from *Diary of St Faustina*. The number following each quote refers to the appropriate paragraph numbers used in both the Polish and English editions of the Diary, *Divine Mercy in My Soul*. (*Diary of St Maria Faustina Kowalska*, Stockbridge, Mass. U.S.A. 2006, © Congregation of Marians.)

Marian Fathers

Catholic Prayers

Our Father

Our Father, who art in heaven, hallowed be thy name. Thy Kingdom come. Thy will be done on earth as it is in heaven. Give us this day our daily bread, and forgive us our trespasses, as we forgive those who trespass against us, and lead us not into temptation, but deliver us from evil. Amen.

Hail Mary

Hail, Mary, full of grace, the Lord is with thee: blessed art thou among women, and blessed is the fruit of thy womb, Jesus. Holy Mary, Mother of God, pray for us sinners, now, and at the hour of our death. Amen.

Glory be to the Father

Glory be to the Father, and to the Son, and to the Holy Spirit. As it was in the beginning, is now, and ever shall be, world without end. Amen.

The Apostles' Creed

I believe in God, the Father almighty, creator of heaven and earth. I believe in Jesus Christ, his only Son, our Lord. He was conceived by the power of the Holy Spirit and born of the Virgin Mary. He suffered under Pontius Pilate, was crucified, died, and was buried. He descended to the dead. On the third day he rose again. He ascended into heaven, and is seated at the right hand of the Father. He will come again to judge the living and the dead. I believe in the Holy Spirit, the holy Catholic Church, the communion of saints, the forgiveness of sins, the resurrection of the body, and the life everlasting. Amen.

An Act of Contrition

O my God, I am sorry and beg pardon for all my sins, and detest them above all things, because they deserve your dreadful punishments, because they have crucified my loving Saviour Jesus Christ, and, most of all, because they offend your infinite goodness; and I firmly resolve, by the help of your grace, never to offend you again, and carefully to avoid the occasions of sin.

The Memorare

Remember, O most loving Virgin Mary, that it is a thing unheard of, that anyone ever had recourse to your protection, implored your help, or sought your intercession, and was left forsaken. Filled therefore with confidence in your goodness I fly to you, O Mother, Virgin of virgins. To you I come, before you I stand, a sorrowful sinner. Despise not my poor words, O Mother of the Word of God, but graciously hear and grant my prayer.

The Angelus

May be said morning, noon, and night, to put us in mind that God the Son became man for our salvation.

V. The Angel of the Lord declared to Mary:

R. And she conceived of the Holy Spirit.
   Hail Mary...

V. Behold the handmaid of the Lord:

R. Be it done to me according to your word.
   Hail Mary...

V. And the Word was made Flesh:

R. And dwelt among us.
   Hail Mary...

V. Pray for us, O holy Mother of God.

R. That we may be made worthy of the promises of Christ.

Let us pray:

Pour forth, we beseech you, O Lord, your grace into our hearts, that we, to whom the Incarnation of Christ, your Son, was made known by the message of an angel, may by his passion and cross ✠ be brought to the glory of his resurrection, through the same Christ our Lord. R. Amen.

The Regina Caeli

V. O Queen of heaven, rejoice! Alleluia,

R. For he whom you did merit to bear, Alleluia,

V. Has risen as he said. Alleluia,

R. Pray for us to God. Alleluia,

V. Rejoice and be glad, O Virgin Mary, Alleluia,
R. For the Lord has risen indeed, Alleluia.

Let us pray:
God our Father, you give joy to the world by the resurrection of your Son, our Lord Jesus Christ. Through the prayers of his mother, the Virgin Mary, bring us to the happiness of eternal life. We ask this through our Lord Jesus Christ, your Son, who lives and reigns with you and the Holy Spirit, one God, for ever and ever. R. Amen.

The Hail Holy Queen

Hail, holy Queen, mother of mercy; hail, our life, our sweetness, and our hope! To you do we cry, poor banished children of Eve; to you do we send up our sighs, mourning and weeping in this vale of tears. Turn then, most gracious advocate, your eyes of mercy towards us; and after this our exile, show to us the blessed fruit of your womb, Jesus. O clement, O loving, O sweet Virgin Mary.

V. Pray for us, O holy Mother of God.
R. That we may be made worthy of the promises of Christ.

Let us pray:
O God, whose only-begotten Son, by his life, death and resurrection, has purchased for us the rewards of eternal life; grant, we beseech you, that meditating on these Mysteries of the most holy Rosary of the Blessed Virgin

Mary, we may both imitate what they contain, and obtain
what they promise, through the same Christ our Lord.
R. Amen.

The Litany to the Sacred Heart of Jesus

V. Lord, have mercy on us.
R. Christ, have mercy on us.
V. Lord, have mercy on us.
R. Christ, graciously hear us.

God the Father of Heaven, *have mercy on us (repeat)*.
God the Son, Redeemer of the world.
God the Holy Spirit.
Holy Trinity, one God.
Heart of Jesus, Son of the Eternal Father.
Heart of Jesus, formed by the Holy Spirit in the Virgin
  Mother's womb.
Heart of Jesus, substantially united to the Word of God.
Heart of Jesus, of infinite majesty.
Heart of Jesus, holy temple of God.
Heart of Jesus, tabernacle of the Most High.
Heart of Jesus, house of God and gate of heaven.
Heart of Jesus, glowing furnace of charity.
Heart of Jesus, vessel of justice and love.
Heart of Jesus, full of goodness and love.
Heart of Jesus, abyss of all virtues.
Heart of Jesus, most worthy of all praise.
Heart of Jesus, King and centre of all hearts.

Heart of Jesus, in whom are all the treasures of wisdom
and knowledge.

Heart of Jesus, in whom dwells all the fullness of the
Godhead.

Heart of Jesus, in whom the Father was well pleased.

Heart of Jesus, of whose fullness we have all received.

Heart of Jesus, desire of the everlasting hills.

Heart of Jesus, patient and rich in mercy.

Heart of Jesus, rich to all who call upon You.

Heart of Jesus, fount of life and holiness.

Heart of Jesus, propitiation for our offences.

Heart of Jesus, overwhelmed with reproaches.

Heart of Jesus, bruised for our iniquities.

Heart of Jesus, obedient even unto death.

Heart of Jesus, pierced with a lance.

Heart of Jesus, source of all consolation.

Heart of Jesus, our life and resurrection.

Heart of Jesus, our peace and reconciliation.

Heart of Jesus, victim for our sins.

Heart of Jesus, salvation of those who hope in You.

Heart of Jesus, hope of those who die in You.

Heart of Jesus, delight of all saints.

V. Lamb of God, who takest away the sins of the world,
R. spare us, O Lord.

V. Lamb of God, who takest away the sins of the world,
R. graciously hear us, O Lord.

V. Lamb of God, who takest away the sins of the world,

R. have mercy on us.

V. Jesus, meek and humble of Heart,

R. make our hearts like unto Thine.

Let us pray:

Almighty and eternal God, look upon the Heart of Thy most beloved Son and upon the praises and satisfaction which He offers Thee in the name of sinners; and to those who implore Thy mercy, in Thy great goodness, grant forgiveness in the name of the same Jesus Christ, Thy Son, who lives and reigns with Thee forever and ever. R. Amen.

The Litany of the Blessed Virgin Mary

Lord have mercy.

Lord have mercy.

Christ have mercy.

Christ have mercy.

Lord have mercy.

Lord have mercy.

Christ hear us.

Christ graciously hear us.

God the Father of heaven,

have mercy on us. (repeat)

God the Son, Redeemer of the world,

God the Holy Spirit,

Holy Trinity, one God,

Holy Mary,

pray for us. (repeat)

Holy Mother of God,

Holy Virgin of virgins,

Mother of Christ,

Mother of divine grace,

Mother most pure,

Mother most chaste,

Mother inviolate,

Mother undefiled,

Mother most lovable,

Mother most admirable,

Mother of good counsel,

Mother of our Creator,

Mother of our Saviour,

Virgin most prudent,
Virgin most venerable,
Virgin most renowned,
Virgin most powerful,
Virgin most merciful,
Virgin most faithful,

Mirror of justice,
Seat of wisdom,
Cause of our joy,
Spiritual vessel,
Vessel of honour,
Singular vessel of devotion,
Mystical rose,
Tower of David,
Tower of ivory,
House of gold,
Ark of the covenant,
Gate of heaven,

Morning Star,
Health of the sick,
Refuge of sinners,
Comfort of the afflicted,
Help of Christians,
Queen of Angels,
Queen of Patriarchs,
Queen of Prophets,
Queen of Apostles
Queen of Martyrs,
Queen of Confessors,
Queen of Virgins,
Queen of all Saints,
Queen conceived
without original sin,
Queen assumed into heaven,
Queen of the most
holy Rosary,
Queen of the Family.
Queen of Peace,

Lamb of God, you take away the sins of the world,
Spare us, O Lord.
Lamb of God, you take away the sins of the world,
Graciously hear us, O Lord.
Lamb of God, you take away the sins of the world,
Have mercy on us.

The Litany to St Joseph

Lord have mercy.
Lord have mercy.
Christ have mercy.
Christ have mercy.
Lord have mercy.
Lord have mercy.
Christ hear us.
Christ graciously hear us.

God the Father of heaven,
have mercy on us. (repeat)
God the Son, Redeemer of the world,
God the Holy Spirit,
Holy Trinity, one God,

Holy Mary,
pray for us. (repeat)
St Joseph,
Renowned offspring of David,
Light of Patriarchs,
Spouse of the Mother of God,

Chaste guardian of the Virgin,
Foster father of the Son of God,
Diligent protector of Christ,
Head of the Holy Family,
Joseph most just,
Joseph most chaste,
Joseph most prudent,
Joseph most strong,
Joseph most obedient,
Joseph most faithful,
Mirror of patience,
Lover of poverty,
Model of artisans,
Glory of home life,
Guardian of virgins,
Pillar of families,
Solace of the wretched,
Hope of the sick,
Patron of the dying,
Terror of demons,
Protector of Holy Church,

Lamb of God, you take away the sins of the world,
Spare us, O Lord.
Lamb of God, you take away the sins of the world,
Graciously hear us, O Lord.
Lamb of God, you take away the sins of the world,
Have mercy on us.

V. He made him the lord of his household.
R. And prince over all his possessions.

Let us pray:
O God, in your ineffable providence you were pleased to choose Blessed Joseph to be the spouse of your most holy Mother; grant, we beg you, that we may be worthy to have him for our intercessor in heaven whom on earth we venerate as our Protector: You who live and reign forever and ever. R. Amen.

The Litany to All Saints

Lord have mercy.
Lord have mercy.
Christ have mercy.
Christ have mercy.
Lord have mercy.
Lord have mercy.
Christ hear us.
Christ graciously hear us.

God the Father of heaven,

have mercy on us. (repeat)
God the Son, Redeemer of the world,
God the Holy Spirit,
Holy Trinity, one God,

Holy Mary,
pray for us. (repeat)
Holy Mother of God,
Holy Virgin of virgins,

St Michael,
St Gabriel,
St Raphael,
All you Holy Angels and
  Archangels,
St John the Baptist,
St Joseph,
All you Holy Patriarchs
  and Prophets,

St Peter,
St Paul,
St Andrew,
St James,
St John,
St Thomas,
St James,
St Philip,
St Bartholomew,
St Matthew,
St Simon,
St Jude,
St Matthias,
St Barnabas,
St Luke,
St Mark,
All you holy Apostles and
  Evangelists,

All you holy Disciples of
  the Lord,
All you holy Innocents,

St Stephen,
St Lawrence,
St Vincent,
Ss Fabian and Sebastian,
Ss John and Paul,
Ss Cosmos and Damian,
All you holy Martyrs,

St Sylvester,
St Gregory,
St Ambrose,
St Augustine,
St Jerome,
St Martin,
St Nicholas,
All you holy Bishops and
  Confessors,
All you holy Doctors,

St Anthony,
St Benedict,
St Bernard,
St Dominic,
St Francis,

All you holy Priests and Levites,

All you holy Monks and Hermits,

St Mary Magdalene,

St Agatha,

St Lucy,

St Agnes,

St Cecilia,

St Anastasia,

St Catherine,

St Clare,

All you holy Virgins and Widows,

All you holy Saints of God,

Lord, be merciful,

Lord save your people, (repeat)

From all evil,

From all sin,

From your wrath,

From a sudden and unprovided death,

From the snares of the devil,

From anger, hatred, and all ill-will,

From the spirit of uncleanness,

From lightning and tempest,

From the scourge of earthquake,

From plague, famine, and war,

From everlasting death,

By the mystery of your holy Incarnation,

By your Coming,

By your Birth,

By your Baptism and holy fasting,

By your Cross and Passion,

By your Death and Burial,

By your holy Resurrection,

By your wonderful Ascension,

By the coming of the Holy Spirit,

On the day of judgment,

Be merciful to us sinners,

Lord, hear our prayer, (repeat)

That you will spare us,

That you will pardon us,

That it may please you to bring us to true penance,
Guide and protect your holy Church,
Preserve in holy religion the Pope, and all those in holy
    Orders,
Humble the enemies of holy Church,
Give peace and unity to the whole Christian people,
Bring back to the unity of the Church all
    those who are straying, and bring all
    unbelievers to the light of the Gospel,
Strengthen and preserve us in your holy service,
Raise our minds to desire the things of heaven,
Reward all our benefactors with eternal blessings,
Deliver our souls from eternal damnation,
    and the souls of our brethren, relatives,
    and benefactors,
Give and preserve the fruits of the earth,
Grant eternal rest to all the faithful departed,
That it may please You to hear and heed
    us, Jesus, Son of the Living God,

Lamb of God, you take away the sins of the world,
Spare us, O Lord.
Lamb of God, you take away the sins of the world,
Graciously hear us, O Lord.
Lamb of God, you take away the sins of the world,
Have mercy on us.
Christ, hear us,

Christ, graciously hear us
Lord Jesus, hear our prayer.
Lord Jesus, hear our prayer.
Lord, have mercy on us.
Lord, have mercy on us.
Christ, have mercy on us.
Christ, have mercy on us.
Lord, have mercy on us.
Lord, have mercy on us.

Message and Devotion to the Divine Mercy

Trust

Trust in Jesus is the essence of the message and devotion to the Divine Mercy. When we go to a public fountain, we can draw water from it as long as we have a vessel or container of some kind to put the water in. If our vessel is small, we can only bring back a little water; if it's large, we can bring back a lot. And anyone with a vessel can draw water from the fountain. The water is there for us, and no one is excluded. All we need is a vessel.

So it is with God's Mercy. In repeated revelations to St Faustina, Our Divine Saviour makes it clear that the fountain is His Heart, the water is His mercy, and the vessel is trust.

I have opened My Heart as a living fountain of mercy. Let all souls draw life from it. Let them approach this sea of mercy with great trust. (1520) I am offering people a vessel with which they are to keep coming for graces to the fountain of mercy. That vessel is this image with the signature: Jesus, I trust in You. (327) The graces of My mercy are drawn by means of one vessel only, and that is - trust. The more a soul trusts, the more it will receive. (1578)

In the *Diary* of St Faustina, we hear Our Lord reminding us that we should depend upon His love... that He alone is worthy of our trust:

> I never reject a contrite heart. (1485) Sooner would heaven and earth turn into nothingness than would My mercy not embrace a trusting soul. (1777)

But there is more to trust than just believing that God is trustworthy. We have to act upon that belief. Trust involves a turning back to God, a real conversion of our whole lives to God, repenting of our sins and forgiving others. Trust is a living faith. Trust means that we agree to let God be God, instead of trying to be God ourselves. (Trust is the antidote to the first sin of Adam!) It means that we agree that God can write the script of our lives, instead of insisting on our own script. It means that we agree with the great pledge we make in the Our Father: "Your will [not mine] be done on earth as it is in heaven." It means that even in our moments of agony we agree with the cry of Jesus in the Garden, "Not my will, but Yours be done." (*Lk* 22:42)

Mercy

In St Faustina's *Diary*, Christ spoke to her about the importance of mercy - not just occasionally celebrating the feast, but living God's Mercy in our lives:

> My daughter, if I demand through you that people revere My mercy, you should be the first to distinguish

yourself by this confidence in My mercy. I demand from you deeds of mercy, which are to arise out of love for Me. You are to show mercy to your neighbours always and everywhere. You must not shrink from this or try to excuse or absolve yourself from it.

I am giving you three ways of exercising mercy toward your neighbour: the first - by deed, the second - by word, the third - by prayer. In these three degrees is contained the fullness of mercy, and it is an unquestionable proof of love for Me. By this means a soul glorifies and pays reverence to My mercy. Yes, the first Sunday after Easter is the Feast of Mercy, but there must also be acts of mercy, and I demand the worship of My mercy through the solemn celebration of the Feast and through the veneration of the image which is painted. By means of this image I shall grant many graces to souls. It is to be a reminder of the demands of My mercy, because even the strongest faith is of no avail without works. (742)

Later, St Faustina describes her understanding of Christ's words to her:

For there are three ways of performing an act of mercy: the merciful word, by forgiving and by comforting; secondly, if you can offer no word, then pray - that too is mercy; and thirdly, deeds of mercy.

And when the Last Day comes, we shall be judged
from this, and on this basis we shall receive the eternal
verdict. (1158)

God is Mercy itself, and we are called to practice the
ABC's of mercy (*A*sk for His Mercy, *B*e merciful to others,
*C*ompletely trust in Jesus). The trust in Jesus is the vital
ingredient. We do not simply ask for mercy, nor do we
simply try to be good to other people. We ask with
complete trust, and Our Lord fills us with grace so that we
can be merciful as our Heavenly Father is merciful.

On this foundation - Trust in God and mercy towards
others - are based forms of the devotion to the Divine Mercy
given by Jesus to Sister Faustina: The Feast of Mercy, The
Image of the Merciful Jesus, The Chaplet, The Hour of
Mercy and spreading the devotion to the Divine Mercy.

The Feast of the Divine Mercy
(Divine Mercy Sunday)

Among all of the elements of devotion to the Divine
Mercy requested by our Lord through St Faustina
Kowalska, the Feast of Mercy holds first place. The
Lord's will with regard to its establishment was already
made known in His first revelation to the saint, as
recorded in her Diary. In all, there were 14 revelations
concerning the desired feast. The most comprehensive
revelation can be found in *Diary* entry 699:

My daughter, tell the whole world about My inconceivable mercy. I desire that the Feast of Mercy be a refuge and shelter for all souls, and especially for poor sinners. On that day the very depths of My tender mercy are open. I pour out a whole ocean of graces upon those souls who approach the fount of My mercy. The soul that will go to Confession and receive Holy Communion shall obtain complete forgiveness of sins and punishment. On that day all the divine floodgates through which grace flow are opened. Let no soul fear to draw near to Me, even though its sins be as scarlet. My mercy is so great that no mind, be it of man or of angel, will be able to fathom it throughout all eternity. Everything that exists has come forth from the very depths of My most tender mercy. Every soul in its relation to Me will contemplate My love and mercy throughout eternity. The Feast of Mercy emerged from My very depths of tenderness. It is My desire that it be solemnly celebrated on the first Sunday after Easter. Mankind will not have peace until it turns to the Fount of My Mercy.

Our Lord's explicit desire is that this feast be celebrated on the first Sunday after Easter. This Sunday is designated in the liturgy as the Octave Day of Easter. It was officially called the Second Sunday of Easter after the liturgical reform of Vatican II. Now, by the Decree of the

Congregation for Divine Worship and the Discipline of the Sacraments, the name of this liturgical day has been changed to: Second Sunday of Easter, or Divine Mercy Sunday. Pope John Paul II made the surprise announcement of this change in his homily at the canonisation of St Faustina on 30th April, 2000. There, he declared: "It is important then that we accept the whole message that comes to us from the word of God on this Second Sunday of Easter, which from now on throughout the Church, will be called *Divine Mercy Sunday*."

By the words "the whole message," Pope John Paul II was referring to the connection between the "Easter Mystery of the Redemption" - in other words, the suffering, death, burial, resurrection, and ascension of Christ, followed by the sending of the Holy Spirit - and this Feast of Divine Mercy, the Octave Day of Easter, which fulfils the grace of atonement as lived through by Christ Jesus and offered to all who come to Him with trust.

Clearly, Divine Mercy Sunday is not a new feast established to celebrate St Faustina's revelations. Indeed, it is not primarily about St Faustina at all - nor is it altogether a new feast! The title "Divine Mercy Sunday" does highlight and amplify the meaning of the day. In this way, it recovers an ancient liturgical tradition, reflected in a teaching attributed to St Augustine about the Easter Octave, which he called "the days of mercy and pardon," and the Octave Day itself "the compendium of the days of mercy."

Liturgically the Easter Octave has always been centered on the theme of Divine Mercy and forgiveness. Divine Mercy Sunday, therefore, point us to the merciful love of God that lies behind the whole Paschal Mystery - the whole mystery of the death, burial and resurrection of Christ - made present for us in the Eucharist. In this way, it also sums up the whole Easter Octave. As Pope John Paul II pointed out in his *Regina Caeli* address on Divine Mercy Sunday, 1995: "the whole Octave of Easter is like a single day," and the Octave Sunday is meant to be the day of "thanksgiving for the goodness God has shown to man in the whole Easter mystery."

Given the liturgical appropriateness of the title "Divine Mercy Sunday" for the Octave Day of Easter, therefore, the Holy See did not give this title to the Second Sunday of Easter merely as an "option," for those dioceses who happen to like that sort of thing! Rather, the decree issued on 5th May, 2000, by the Sacred Congregation for Divine Worship and the Discipline of the Sacraments clearly states: "the Supreme Pontiff John Paul II has graciously determined that in the Roman Missal, after the title Second Sunday of Easter, there shall henceforth be added the appellation 'or [that is] Divine Mercy Sunday'…".

How to prepare to and celebrate Divine Mercy Sunday

Jesus asked Sr Faustina to pray the special novena as a preparation to the Feast of the Divine Mercy:

> I desire that during these nine days you bring souls to the fountain of My mercy, that they may draw there from strength and refreshment and whatever grace they have need of in the hardships of life, and especially at the hour of death. (1209)

The novena to the Divine Mercy (*see p.61*) is typically nine days of prayer with a specific Intention for each day and followed by the Chaplet. The Chaplet can be said anytime, but the Lord specifically asked that it be recited as a novena. He promised:

> By this Novena (of Chaplets), I will grant every possible grace to souls. (796)

Thus, to fittingly observe the Feast of Mercy, we should:

1. Celebrate the Feast on the Sunday after Easter;
2. Sincerely repent of all our sins;
3. Place our complete trust in Jesus;
4. Go to confession, preferably before that Sunday;
5. Receive Holy Communion on the day of the Feast;
6. Venerate the Image of the Divine Mercy;
7. Be merciful to others, through our actions, words, and prayers on their behalf.

The Image of the Merciful Jesus

In 1931, our Lord appeared to St Faustina in a vision. She saw Jesus clothed in a white garment with His right hand raised in blessing. His left hand was touching His garment in the area of the Heart, from where two large rays came forth, one red and the other pale. She gazed intently at the Lord in silence, her soul filled with awe, but also with great joy. Jesus said to her:

Paint an image according to the pattern you see, with the signature: Jesus, I trust in You... I promise that the soul that will venerate this image will not perish. I also promise victory over [its] enemies already here on earth, especially at the hour of death. I Myself will defend it as My own glory. (47, 48) I am offering people a vessel with which they are to keep coming for graces to the fountain of mercy. That vessel is this image with the signature: Jesus, I trust in You (327). I desire that this image be venerated, first in your chapel, and [then] throughout the world. (47)

At the request of her spiritual director, St Faustina asked the Lord about the meaning of the rays in the image. She heard these words in reply:

The two rays denote Blood and Water. The pale ray stands for the Water which makes souls righteous. The red ray stands for the Blood which is the life of souls... These two rays issued forth from the depths of My tender mercy when My agonized Heart was opened by a lance on the Cross... Happy is the one who will dwell in their shelter, for the just hand of God shall not lay hold of him. (299) By means of this image I shall grant many graces to souls. It is to be a reminder of the demands of My mercy, because even the strongest faith is of no avail without works. (742)

These words indicate that the Image represents the graces of Divine Mercy poured out upon the world, especially through Baptism and the Eucharist.

Many different versions of this image have been painted, but our Lord made it clear that the painting itself is not what is important. When St Faustina first saw the original image that was being painted under her direction by Eugeniusz Kazimirowski in Vilnius in 1934, she wept in disappointment and complained to Jesus: Who will paint You as beautiful as You are? (313). In answer, she heard these words:

Not in the beauty of the colour, nor of the brush lies the greatness of this image, but in My grace. (313)

So no matter which version of the Image we prefer, we can be assured that it is a vehicle of God's grace, if it is revered with trust in His mercy.

The Chaplet to the Divine Mercy

In 1935, St Faustina received a vision of an angel sent by God to chastise a certain city. She began to pray for mercy, but her prayers were powerless. Suddenly she saw the Holy Trinity and felt the power of Jesus' grace within her. At the same time she found herself pleading with God for mercy with words she heard interiorly:

> Eternal Father, I offer You the Body and Blood, Soul and Divinity of Your dearly beloved Son, Our Lord Jesus Christ, in atonement for our sins and those of the whole world; for the sake of His sorrowful Passion, have mercy on us. (475)

As she continued saying this inspired prayer, the angel became helpless and could not carry out the deserved punishment (see 474). The next day, as she was entering the chapel, she again heard this interior voice, instructing her how to recite the prayer that our Lord later called "the Chaplet." This time, after "have mercy on us" were added the words "and on the whole world" (476). From then on, she recited this form of prayer almost constantly, offering it especially for the dying.

In subsequent revelations, the Lord made it clear that the Chaplet *(see p.60)* was not just for her, but for the whole world. He also attached extraordinary promises to its recitation:

> Encourage souls to say the Chaplet which I have given you... (1541) Whoever will recite it will receive great mercy at the hour of death. (687) When they say this Chaplet in the presence of the dying, I will stand between My Father and the dying person, not as the just Judge but as the Merciful Saviour. (1541) Priests

will recommend it to sinners as their last hope of salvation. Even if there were a sinner most hardened, if he were to recite this Chaplet only once, he would receive grace from My infinite mercy (687). Through the Chaplet you will obtain everything, if what you ask for is compatible with My will. (1731)

The Hour of Mercy - "Three O'clock Prayer"

In His revelations to St Faustina, Our Lord asked for a special prayer and meditation on His Passion each afternoon at the three o'clock hour *(see p.71)*, the hour that recalls His death on the cross:

At three o'clock, implore My mercy, especially for sinners; and, if only for a brief moment, immerse yourself in My Passion, particularly in My abandonment at the moment of agony. This is the hour of great mercy... In this hour, I will refuse nothing to the soul that makes a request of Me in virtue of My Passion. (1320)

... as often as you hear the clock strike the third hour, immerse yourself completely in My mercy, adoring and glorifying it; invoke its omnipotence for the whole world, and particularly for poor sinners; for at that moment mercy was opened wide for every soul. In this hour you can obtain everything for yourself and for others for the asking; it was the hour of grace for the whole world - mercy triumphed over justice. (1572)

My daughter, try your best to make the Stations of the Cross in this hour, provided that your duties permit it; and if you are not able to make the Stations of the Cross, then at least step into the chapel for a moment and adore, in the Most Blessed Sacrament, My Heart, which is full of mercy; and should you be unable to step into the chapel, immerse yourself in prayer there where you happen to be, if only for a very brief instant. (1572)

From these detailed instructions, it's clear that Our Lord wants us to turn our attention to His Passion at the three o'clock hour to whatever degree our duties allow, and He wants us to ask for His mercy. We may not all be able to make the Stations or adore Him in the Blessed Sacrament, but we can all mentally pause for a "brief instant," think of His total abandonment at the hour of agony, and say a short prayer such as "Jesus, Mercy," or "Jesus, for the sake of Your sorrowful Passion, have mercy on us and on the whole world." This meditation, however brief, on Christ's Passion brings us face-to-face with the cross, and, as Pope John Paul II writes in his Encyclical Letter *Rich in Mercy*, "It is in the cross that the revelation of merciful love attains its culmination" (8). God invites us, the Holy Father continues, "to have 'mercy' on His only Son, the crucified one". Thus, our reflection on the Passion should lead to a type of love for

Our Lord which is "not only an act of solidarity with the suffering Son of man, but also a kind of 'mercy' shown by each one of us to the Son of the Eternal Father."

Spreading the Divine Mercy Devotion

Jesus said to Sr Faustina:

> Souls who spread the honour of My mercy I shield through their entire lives as a tender mother her infant, and at the hour of death I will not be a Judge for them, but the Merciful Saviour. (1075)

By these words Jesus is encouraging us to spread the worship to the Divine Mercy. He has promise maternal care to those who do so by shielding them throughout their entire life and at the hour of death. He made a singular promise to priests saying:

> Tell My priests that hardened sinners will repent on hearing their words when they speak about My unfathomable mercy, about the compassion I have for them in My Heart. To priests who proclaim and extol My mercy, I will give wondrous power; I will anoint their words and touch the hearts of those to whom they will speak. (1521)

The foundation for the worship and apostolate of Divine Mercy is the testimony of once own life according to the spirit of this devotion; namely, the spirit of childlike confidence in the goodness and omnipotence of God accompanied by an active love of one's neighbour.

Today the Lord said to me... All those souls who will glorify My mercy and spread its worship, encouraging others to trust in My mercy, will not experience terror at the hour of death. My mercy will shield them in that final battle... (1540)

Prayers with St Faustina

THE HOLY ROSARY

*Meditations on the Rosary based
on St Sister Faustina's notes from her Diary*

Introduction

I saw, between heaven and earth, the Mother of God, clothed in a bright robe. She was praying with Her hands folded on Her bosom, Her eyes fixed on Heaven. From Her Heart issued forth fiery rays, some of which were turned toward Heaven while the others were covering our country (33).

O radiant Virgin, pure as crystal, all immersed in God, I offer You my spiritual life; arrange everything that it may be pleasing to Your Son. (844)

Through your hands, Mother of Mercy, I offer this prayer of the Rosary for the intention of the Holy Church, our Homeland and for the grace of repentance for sinners of the whole world...

Part I - the Joyful Mysteries

1. The Annunciation

This immense love and abyss of mercy are made known in the Incarnation. (180) Before every Holy Communion I

earnestly ask the Mother of God to help me prepare my
soul for the coming of Her Son, and I clearly feel Her
protection over me. I entreat Her to be so gracious as to
enkindle in me the fire of God's love, such as burned in
Her own pure heart at the time of the Incarnation of the
Word of God. (1114)

2. The Visitation

Jesus: My daughter, in this meditation, consider the love
of neighbour. Is your love for your neighbour guided by
My love? Do you pray for Your enemies? Do you wish
well to those who have, in one way or another, caused
you sorrow or offended you? Know that whatever good
you do, to any soul, I accept it as if you had done it to
Me. (1768)

3. The Birth of the Child Jesus

When I arrived at Midnight Mass,... I steeped myself in
deep recollection, during which time I saw the stable of
Bethlehem filled with great radiance. The Blessed Virgin,
all lost in the deepest of love, was wrapping Jesus in
swaddling clothes, but Saint Joseph was still asleep. Only
after the Mother of God put Jesus in the manger, did the
light of God awaken Joseph, who also prayed. But after a
while, I was left alone with Infant Jesus who stretched out
His little hands to me, and I understood that I was to take
Him in my arms. Jesus pressed His head against my heart

and gave me to know, by His profound gaze, how good He found it to be next to my heart. (1442)

4. The Presentation of Jesus in the Temple

O Mary, today (because of the prophetic words of Simeon) a terrible sword has pierced Your holy soul. Except for God, no one knows of Your suffering. Your soul does not break; it is brave, because it is with Jesus. Sweet Mother, unite my soul to Jesus, because it is only then that I will be able to endure all trials and tribulations, and only in union with Jesus will my little sacrifices be pleasing to God. Sweetest Mother, continue to teach me about the interior life. May the sword of suffering never break me. O pure Virgin, pour courage into my heart and guard it. (915)

5. The Finding of Jesus in the Temple

I look for no happiness beyond my own interior where God dwells. I rejoice that God dwells within me; here I abide with Him unendingly: it is here that my greatest intimacy with Him exists; here I dwell with Him in safety; here is a place not probed by the human eye. The Blessed Virgin encourages me to commune with God in this way. (454)

Conclusion

O Mary, my Mother and my Lady, I offer You my soul, my body, my life and my death, and all that will follow it. I place everything in Your hands. O my Mother, cover my soul with Your virginal mantle and grant me the grace of purity of heart, soul and body. Defend me with Your power against all enemies. (79)

Part II - The Luminous Mysteries

Introduction

O Light eternal, who came to this earth, enlighten my mind and strengthen my will that I may not give up in times of great affliction. May Your light dissipate all the shadows of doubt. May Your omnipotence act through me. I trust in You, O uncreated Light! (830)

1. The Baptism of Jesus in the Jordan

Once after Holy Communion, I heard these words: 'You are Our dwelling place'. At the moment, I felt in my soul the presence of the Holy Trinity, the Father, the Son and the Holy Spirit. I felt that I was the temple of God. I felt I was a child of the Father. I cannot explain all this, but the spirit understands it well. O infinite Goodness, how low You stoop to Your miserable creature! (451). Thank You, God, for Holy Baptism which engrafted me into Your family, a gift great beyond all thought or expression which transforms my soul. (1286)

2. Jesus Reveals His Glory at the Wedding of Cana

I remained alone with the Most Holy Mother who instructed me about the will of God and how to apply it to my life, submitting completely to His most holy decrees. It is impossible for one to please God without obeying His holy will. 'My daughter, I strongly recommend that you faithfully fulfil all God's wishes, for that is most pleasing in His holy eyes. I very much desire that you distinguish yourself in this faithfulness in accomplishing God's will. Put the will of God before all sacrifices and holocausts.' (1244)

3. The Proclamation of the Kingdom of God

The Lord said to me, 'Do not tire of proclaiming My mercy'. O Eternal Love, I want all the souls You have created to come to know You. I would like to be a priest, for then I would speak without cease about Your mercy to sinful souls drowned in despair. I would like to be a missionary and carry the light of faith to savage nations in order to make You known to souls, and to be completely consumed for them and to die a martyr's death, just as You died for them and for me. O Jesus, I know only too well that I can be a priest, a missionary, a preacher, and that I can die a martyr's death by completely emptying and denying myself for love of You, O Jesus and of immortal souls. (1521, 302)

4. The Transfiguration of Jesus

My Jesus, penetrate me through and through so that I might be able to reflect You in my whole life. Divinize me so that my deeds may have supernatural value. I want to be completely transformed into Your mercy and to be Your reflection, O Lord. May the greatest of all divine attributes, that of Your unfathomable mercy, pass through my heart and soul to my neighbour. (...) O my Jesus, transform me into Yourself, for you can do all things. (1242, 163)

5. The Institution of the Eucharist

Today during Holy Mass I saw the Crucified Jesus. Jesus was nailed to the cross and was in great agony. His suffering pierced me, soul and body, in a manner which was invisible, but nevertheless most painful. (...) Oh, what awesome mysteries take place during Mass! With what great devotion should we listen to and take part in this death of Jesus. One day we will know what God is doing for us in each Mass, and what sort of gift He is preparing in it for us. Only His divine love could permit that such a gift be provided for us. (913-914)

Conclusion

Jesus, source of life, sanctify me. O my strength, fortify me. My Commander, fight for me. Only light of my soul, enlighten me. My Master, guide me. I entrust myself to You, as a little child does to its mother's love. Even if all things were to conspire against me, and even if the ground were to give way under my feet, I would be at peace close to Your heart. (1490)

Part III - The Sorrowful Mysteries

Introduction

Jesus told me that I please Him best by meditating on His sorrowful Passion, and by such meditation much light falls upon my soul. He who wants to learn true humility should reflect upon the Passion of Jesus...

I want to resemble You, O Jesus, - You crucified, tortured and humiliated. Jesus, imprint upon my heart and soul Your own humility. I love You, Jesus, to the point of madness, You who were crushed with suffering as described by the prophet. (cf. *Is* 53:2-9) (267)

1. The Agony of Jesus in the Garden

In the evening, when I entered the small chapel, I heard these words in my soul: My daughter, consider these words: "And being in agony, He prayed more earnestly." When I started to think about them more deeply, much light streamed into my soul. I learned how much we need perseverance in prayer and that our salvation often depends on such difficult prayer. (157)

2. The Scourging of Jesus at the Pillar

I saw how the Lord Jesus suffered as He was being scourged. Oh, such an inconceivable agony! How terribly Jesus suffered during the scourging! O poor sinners, on the day of judgment how will you face the Jesus whom you are now torturing so cruelly? His blood flowed to the ground, and in some places His flesh started to fall off. I saw a few bare bones on His back. The meek Jesus moaned softly and sighed. (188)

3. The Crowning of Jesus with Thorns

After the scourging, the torturers took the Lord and stripped Him of His own garment, which had already adhered to the wounds; as they took it off, His wounds reopened; then they threw a dirty and tattered scarlet cloak over the fresh wounds of the Lord. The cloak, in some places, barely reached His knees. They made Him sit on a piece of beam. And then they wove a crown of thorns, which they put on His sacred head. They put a reed in His hand and made fun of Him, bowing to Him, as to a king. Some spat in His face, while others took the reed and struck Him on the head with it. Others caused Him pain by slapping Him; still others covered His face and struck Him with their fists. Jesus bore all this with meekness... They tried to outdo each other in insulting the Lord. I reflected: Where does such malice in man come from? It is caused by sin. Love and sin have met. (408)

4. Jesus Carries His Heavy Cross

The world still has no idea of all that Jesus suffered. I accompanied Him to the Garden of Gethsemane; I stayed with Him in the prison; I went with Him before the judges; I underwent with Him each of the tortures. Not a single one of His movements or looks escaped my notice. I came to know all the omnipotence of His love and His mercy toward souls. (1054)

5. The Crucifixion and Death of Jesus

At three o'clock, I saw the Lord Jesus, crucified, who looked at me and said, I thirst. Then I saw two rays issue from His side, just as they appear in the image. I then felt in my soul the desire to save souls and to empty myself for the sake of poor sinners. (648)

Jesus' mortal life was coming to an end. I heard His seven words; then He looked at me and said, Beloved daughter of My Heart, you are My solace amidst terrible torments. (1058)

Conclusion

Mother of God, Your soul was plunged into a sea of bitterness; look upon Your child and teach her to suffer and to love while suffering. Fortify my soul that pain will not break it. Mother of grace, teach me to live by [the power of] God. (315)

Part IV - The Glorious Mysteries

Introduction

O sweet Mother of God, I model my life on You; You are for me the bright dawn; O Mother, Immaculate Virgin, in

You the divine ray is reflected, midst storms, 'tis You who teach me to love the Lord, O my shield and defence from the foe. (1232)

1. The Resurrection of Jesus

Today, during the [Mass of the] Resurrection, I saw the Lord Jesus in the midst of a great light. He approached me and said: Peace be to you, My children, and He lifted up His hand and gave His blessing. The wounds in His hands, feet and side were indelible and shining. When He looked at me with such kindness and love, my whole soul drowned itself in Him. And He said to me, You have taken a great part in My Passion; therefore I now give you a great share in My joy and glory. (205)

2. The Ascension of Jesus into Heaven

Today I accompanied the Lord Jesus as He ascended into heaven... Then I saw myself in the midst of a huge crowd of disciples and apostles, together with the Mother of God. Jesus was telling them to... Go out into the whole world and teach in My name. He stretched out His hands and blessed them and disappeared in a cloud. I saw the longing of Our Lady. Her soul yearned for Jesus with the whole force of Her love. But She was so peaceful and so united to the will of God that there was not a stir in Her heart but for what God wanted. (1710)

3. The Descent of the Holy Spirit

I am reliving those moments with Our Lady. With great longing, I am waiting for the Lord's coming. Great are my desires. I desire that all humankind come to know the Lord. I would like to prepare all nations for the coming of the Word Incarnate. O Jesus, make the fount of Your mercy gush forth more abundantly, for humankind is seriously ill. (793)

4. The Assumption of the Blessed Virgin Mary

During meditation, God's presence pervaded me keenly, and I was aware of the Virgin Mary's joy at the moment of Her Assumption... I remained alone with the Most Holy Mother who instructed me about the will of God and how to apply it to my life, submitting completely to His most holy decrees. (1244) She said, The soul's true greatness is in loving God and in humbling oneself in His presence, completely forgetting oneself and believing oneself to be nothing; because the Lord is great, but He is well-pleased only with the humble; He always opposes the proud. (1711)

5. Coronation of the Blessed Virgin Mary

From the early morning, I felt the nearness of the Blessed Mother. During Holy Mass, I saw Her, so lovely and so beautiful that I have no words to express even a small part of this beauty. She was all [in] white, with a blue sash around Her waist. Her cloak was also blue, and there was a crown on Her head. Marvellous light streamed forth from Her whole figure. She said these words: 'I am the Queen of heaven and earth, but especially the Mother of your' [Congregation]. (805)

Conclusion

Mary, Immaculate Virgin, take me under Your special protection and guard the purity of my soul, heart and body. You are the model and star of my life. (874)

THE STATIONS OF THE CROSS

Based on the Holy Bible and St Faustina's Diary

Introductory prayer

Merciful Lord, my Master, I want to follow You faithfully. I desire to imitate You in my life in a way that will be more and more perfect; therefore, I am praying that, by meditating on Your passion, You will give me the grace of a greater understanding of the mysteries of spiritual life.

Mary, Mother of Mercy, ever faithful to Christ, lead me in the footsteps of the sorrowful passion of your Son and obtain for me the graces necessary to fruitfully observe of this Way of the Cross. I offer it for the intention of: (for example, priests, religious, and all those striving for perfection).

Station I - Jesus is Condemned to Death

"The chief priests and the entire Sanhedrin kept trying to obtain false testimony against Jesus in order to put him to death, but they found none, though many false witnesses came forward" (Mt 26:59-60).

Jesus: Do not be surprised that you are sometimes unjustly accused. I myself first drank this cup of undeserved suffering for the love of you. (28) When I was before Herod, I obtained a grace for you; namely, that you would be able to rise above human scorn and follow faithfully in My footsteps. (1164)

Sr Faustina: We are sensitive to words and quickly want to answer back, without taking any regard as to whether it is God's will that we should speak. A silent soul is strong; no adversities will harm it if it perseveres in silence. The silent soul is capable of attaining the closest union with God. (477)

Merciful Jesus, help me to accept every human judgment and do not let me ever condemn You in my neighbour.

Station II - Jesus Takes up His Cross

"Then Pilate took Jesus and had him scourged. And the soldiers wove a crown of out of thorns and placed it on

his head, and clothed him in a purple cloak, and they came to him and said, 'Hail King of the Jews!' ... Jesus came out, wearing the crown of thorns and the purple cloak. And he [Pilate] said to them, 'Behold, the man!' When the chief priests and the guards saw him they cried out, 'Crucify him, crucify him!' " (Jn 19:1-6)

Jesus: Do not be afraid of sufferings; I am with you. (151). The more you will come to love suffering, My daughter, the purer your love for Me will be. (279)

Sr Faustina: Jesus, I thank You for the little daily crosses, for opposition to my endeavours, for the hardships of communal life, for the misinterpretation of my intentions, for humiliations at the hands of others, for the harsh way in which we are treated, for false suspicions, for poor health and loss of strength, for self-denial, for dying to myself, for lack of recognition in everything, for upsetting of all my plans. (343)

Merciful Jesus, teach me to value the toil of life, sickness, and every suffering; teach me to carry this cross every day with love.

Station III - Jesus Falls the First Time

"We had all gone astray like sheep, each following his own way; but the Lord laid upon him the guilt of us all... And he shall take away the sins of many, and win pardon for their offences." (Is 53:6,12)

Jesus: My daughter, write that involuntary offences of souls do nor hinder My love for them or prevent Me from uniting Myself with them. But voluntary offences, even the smallest, obstruct My graces, and I cannot lavish My gifts on such souls. (1641)

Sr Faustina: O my Jesus, how prone I am to evil, and this forces me to be constantly vigilant. But I do not lose heart. I trust God's grace, which abounds in the worst misery. (606) Merciful Lord, save me from every voluntary and conscious infidelity, even the smallest.

Station IV - Jesus Meets His Blessed Mother

"Behold, this child is destined for the fall and rise of many in Israel, and to be a sign that will be contradicted - and a sword will pierce your own soul too." (Lk 2:34-35)

Jesus: Listen, My daughter, although all the works that come into being by My will are exposed to great sufferings, consider whether any of them has been subject to greater difficulties than that work which is directly Mine - the work of Redemption. You should not worry too much about adversities. (1643)

Sr Faustina: I saw the Blessed Virgin... (she) held me close to herself and said to me: Be courageous. Do not fear apparent obstacles, but fix your gaze upon the Passion of My Son, and in this way, you will be victorious. (449)

Mary, Mother of Mercy, be with me always, and especially in suffering, in the same way as you were on the way of the cross of your Son.

Station V - Simon of Cyrene Helps Jesus to Carry the Cross

"As they led him away they took hold of a certain Simon, a Cyrenian who was coming in from the country; and after laying the cross on him, they made him carry it behind Jesus." (Lk 23:26)

Jesus: I permit these adversities in order to increase his merit. I do not reward for good results but for the patience and hardship undergone for My sake. (86)

Sr Faustina: O my Jesus, You do not give a reward for the successful performance of a work, but for the good will and labour undertaken. Therefore, I am completely at peace, even if all my undertakings and efforts should be thwarted or should come to naught. If I do all that is in my power, the rest is not my business. (952)

O Jesus, my Lord, let every thought, word and action be undertaken exclusively out of love for You. Purify my intentions.

Station VI - Veronica Wipes the Face of Jesus

"There was in him no stately bearing to make us look at him, nor appearance that would attract us to him. He was spurned and avoided by men, a man of suffering, accustomed to infirmity, one of those from whom men hide their faces, spurned, and we held him in no esteem." (*Is* 53:2-3)

Jesus: Know that whatever good you do to any soul, I accept it as if you had done it to Me. (1768)

Sr Faustina: I am learning how to be good from Jesus, from Him who is goodness itself, so that I may be called a daughter of the heavenly Father. (669) Great love can change small things into great ones, and it is only love which lends value to our actions. (303)

Lord Jesus, my Master, make merciful my eyes, hands, lips, heart... Keep transforming me into mercy.

Station VII - Jesus Falls a Second Time

"Yet it was our infirmities that he bore, our sufferings that he endured, while we thought of him as stricken, as one smitten by God and afflicted." (*Is* 53:4)

Jesus: The cause of your falls is that you rely too much upon yourself and too little on Me. (1488) Without special help from Me, you are not even capable of accepting My graces. (738)

Sr Faustina: Jesus, do not leave me alone... You know, Lord, how weak I am. I am an abyss of wretchedness, I am nothingness itself; so what will be so strange if You leave me alone and I fall? (1489) So You, Jesus, must stand by me constantly like a mother by a helpless child - and even more so. (264)

May Your grace assist me, Lord, so that I may not keep falling continuously into the same errors; and when I fall, help me to get up and praise Your mercy.

Station VIII - Jesus Meets the Women of Jerusalem

"A large crowd of people followed Jesus, including many women who mourned and lamented him. Jesus turned to them and said. 'Daughters of Jerusalem, do not weep for me; weep instead for yourselves.'" (Lk 23:27-28)

Jesus: O how pleasing to Me is living faith! (1420) I desire that you would all have more faith at the present time (352).

Sr Faustina: I fervently beg the Lord to strengthen my faith, so that in my drab, everyday life I will not be guided by human dispositions, but by those of the spirit. Oh, how everything drags man towards the earth! But lively faith maintains the soul in the higher regions and assigns self-love its proper place; that is to say, the lowest one. (210)

Merciful Lord, I thank You for holy baptism and the grace of faith. Again and again I call: Lord, I believe! Increase my faith!

Station IX - Jesus Falls the Third Time

"Though he was harshly treated, he submitted and opened not his mouth. Like a lamb led to the slaughter or a sheep before the shearers, he was silent and opened not his mouth... But the Lord was pleased to crush him in infirmity." (Is 53:7-10)

Jesus: My child, know that the greatest obstacles to holiness are discouragement and an exaggerated anxiety. These will deprive you of the ability to practice virtue... I am always ready to forgive you. As often as you beg for it, you glorify My mercy. (1488)

Sr Faustina: My Jesus, despite Your graces, I see and feel all my misery. I begin my day with battle and end it with battle. As soon as I conquer one obstacle, ten more appear to take its place. But I am not worried, because I know that this is the time of struggle, not peace. (606)

Merciful Lord, I give You this, which is exclusively my own property, that is, sin and human weakness. I beg of You, let my wretchedness be drowned in Your unfathomable mercy.

Station X - Jesus is Stripped of his Garments

"When the soldiers... took his clothes and divided them into four shares, a share for each soldier. They also took his tunic, but the tunic was seamless, woven in one piece from the top down. So they said to one another. 'Let's not tear it but cast lots for it to see whose it will be', in order that the passage of the scripture might be fulfilled." (*Jn* 19:23-24)

Sr Faustina: Jesus was suddenly standing before me, stripped of His clothes, His body completely covered with wounds, His eyes flooded with tears and blood. His face disfigured and covered with spittle. The Lord then said to me:

Jesus: The bride must resemble her Betrothed.

Sr Faustina: I understood these words to their very depth. There is no room for doubt here. My likeness to Jesus must be through suffering and humility. (268)

Jesus, gentle and humble of Heart, touch my heart and make it like Your own.

Station XI - Jesus is Nailed to the Cross

"Those passing by reviled him, shaking their heads and saying, 'You who would destroy the temple and rebuild it in three days, save yourself if you are the Son of God, (and) come down from the cross!' Likewise the chief priests with the scribes and elders mocked him and said

'He saved others; he cannot save himself... He trusted in God; let him deliver him now if he wants him'." (*Mt* 27:39-43)

Jesus: My pupil, have great love for those who cause you suffering. Do good to those who hate you. (1628)

Sr Faustina: O my Jesus, you know what efforts are needed to live sincerely and unaffectedly with those from whom our nature flees, or with those who, deliberately or not, have made us suffer. Humanly speaking, this is impossible. At such times more than at others, I try to discover the Lord Jesus in such a person and for this same Jesus, I do everything for such people. (766)

O purest Love, rule in all Your plenitude in my heart and let me love even the things that, humanly speaking, are impossible to love.

Station XII - Jesus Dies on the Cross

"It was now about noon and darkness came over the whole land until three in the afternoon... Jesus cried out in a loud voice, 'Father, into your hands, I commend my spirit'; and when he had said this he breathed his last" (*Lk* 23:44-46). *"But when they came to Jesus and saw that he was already dead, they did not break his legs, but one soldier thrust his lance into his side, and immediately blood and water flowed out."* (*Jn* 19:33-40)

Jesus: All this is for the salvation of souls. Consider well, My daughter, what you are doing for their salvation. (1184)

Sr Faustina: Then I saw the Lord nailed to the cross. When He had hung on it for a while, I saw a multitude of souls crucified like Him. Then I saw a second multitude of souls, and a third. The second multitude were not nailed to [their] crosses, but were holding them firmly in their hands. The third were neither nailed to [their] crosses, nor holding them firmly in their hands, but were dragging [their] crosses behind them and were discontent. Jesus then said to me:

Jesus: Do you see these souls? Those who are like Me in the pain and contempt they suffer will be like Me also in glory. And those who also resemble Me less in pain and contempt will also bear less resemblance to Me in glory. (446)

O Jesus, my Saviour, hide me in the depth of Your Heart, so that strengthened by Your grace, I may imitate You in the love of the cross and participate in Your glory.

Station XIII - Jesus is Taken Down from the Cross

"The centurion who witnessed what had happened glorified God and said, 'This man was innocent beyond doubt.' When all the people who had gathered for this spectacle saw what had happened, they returned home beating their breasts; but all his acquaintances stood at a distance." (Lk 23:47-49)

Jesus: Most dear to Me is the soul that strongly believes in My goodness and has complete trust in Me. I heap My confidence upon it and give it all it asks. (453)

Sr Faustina: I fly to Your mercy, Compassionate God, who alone are good. Although my misery is great, and my offences are many, I trust in Your mercy, because You are the God of mercy; and, from time immemorial, it has never been heard of, nor do heaven or earth remember, that a soul trusting in Your mercy has been disappointed. (1730)

Merciful Jesus, every day increase within me trust in Your mercy, so I may always and everywhere give witness to Your infinite goodness and love.

Station XIV - Jesus is Laid in the Tomb

"They took the body of Jesus and bound it with the burial cloths along with the spices, according to the Jewish burial custom. Now in the place where he had been crucified there was a garden and in the garden a new tomb, in which no one had yet been buried. So they laid Jesus there because of the Jewish preparation day; for the tomb was close by." (Jn 19:40-42)

Jesus: You are not yet in your homeland; so go, fortified by My grace, and fight for My kingdom in human souls; fight as a king's child would; and remember that the days of your exile will pass quickly, and with them the possibility of earning merit for heaven. I expect from you... a great number of souls who will glorify My mercy for all eternity. (1489)

Sr Faustina: Every soul You have entrusted to me, Jesus, I will try to aid with prayer and sacrifice, so that Your grace can work in them. O great lover of souls, my Jesus, I thank You for the immense confidence with which You have deigned to place souls in our care. (245)

Merciful Lord, grant that not even one of those souls which You have entrusted to me be lost.

Closing Prayer

My Jesus, my only hope, I thank you for this book which You opened to the eyes of my soul. This book is Your Passion, undertaken out of love of me. From this book, I learned how to love God and souls. This book contains inexhaustible treasures. O Jesus, how few souls understand You in Your martyrdom of love. Happy the soul that has come to understand the love of the heart of Jesus. (304)

CHAPLET TO THE DIVINE MERCY

Prayed on ordinary rosary beads, the Chaplet to the Divine Mercy is an intercessory prayer that extends the offering of the Eucharist, so it is especially appropriate to use it after having received Holy Communion at Holy

Mass. It may be said at any time. It is likewise appropriate to pray the Chaplet during the Hour of Great Mercy - Three o'clock each afternoon (recalling the time of Christ's death on the cross).

Begin with the *Our Father...*, the *Hail Mary...*, and the *Apostles' Creed.*

Then, on the five large beads:
Eternal Father, I offer you the Body and Blood, Soul and Divinity, of Your Dearly Beloved Son, Our Lord, Jesus Christ, in atonement for our sins and those of the whole world.

On the ten small beads, say:
For the sake of His sorrowful Passion, have mercy on us and on the whole world.

Conclude with (say 3 times):
Holy God, Holy Mighty One, Holy Immortal One, have mercy on us and on the whole world.

NOVENA TO THE DIVINE MERCY

(Taken from the Diary, 1210 - 1229)

I desire that during these nine days you bring souls to the fount of My mercy, that they may draw from there strength and refreshment and whatever graces they need in the hardships of life and, especially, at the hour of death.

On each day you will bring to My Heart a different group of souls, and you will immerse them in this ocean of My mercy, and I will bring all these souls into the house of My Father. You will do this in this life and in the next. I will deny nothing to any soul whom you will bring to the fount of My mercy. On each day you will beg My Father, on the strength of My bitter Passion, for graces for these souls. (1209)

First Day

Today bring to Me all mankind, especially all sinners, and immerse them in the ocean of My mercy. In this way you will console Me in the bitter grief into which the loss of souls plunges Me.

Most Merciful Jesus, whose very nature it is to have compassion on us and to forgive us, do not look upon our sins but upon our trust which we place in Your infinite goodness. Receive us all into the abode of Your Most Compassionate Heart, and never let us escape from It. We beg this of You by Your love which unites You to the Father and the Holy Spirit.

Eternal Father, turn Your merciful gaze upon all mankind and especially upon poor sinners, all enfolded in the Most Compassionate Heart of Jesus. For the sake of His sorrowful Passion show us Your mercy, that we may praise the omnipotence of Your mercy forever and ever. Amen. *(Then pray the Chaplet to the Divine Mercy)*

Second Day

Today bring to Me the souls of priests and religious, and immerse them in My unfathomable mercy. It was they who gave Me strength to endure My bitter Passion. Through them as through channels My mercy flows out upon mankind.

Most Merciful Jesus, from whom comes all that is good, increase Your grace in men and women consecrated to Your service, that they may perform worthy works of mercy; and that all who see them may glorify the Father of Mercy who is in heaven.

Eternal Father, turn Your merciful gaze upon the company of chosen ones in Your vineyard - upon the souls of priests and religious; and endow them with the strength of Your blessing. For the love of the Heart of Your Son in which they are enfolded, impart to them Your power and light, that they may be able to guide others in the way of salvation and with one voice sing praise to Your boundless mercy for ages without end. Amen.

(Then pray the Chaplet to the Divine Mercy)

Third Day

Today bring to Me all devout and faithful souls, and immerse them in the ocean of My mercy. These souls brought me consolation on the Way of the Cross. They were that drop of consolation in the midst of an ocean of bitterness.

Most Merciful Jesus, from the treasury of Your mercy, You impart Your graces in great abundance to each and all. Receive us into the abode of Your Most Compassionate Heart and never let us escape from It. We beg this grace of You by that most wondrous love for the heavenly Father with which Your Heart burns so fiercely.

Eternal Father, turn Your merciful gaze upon faithful souls, as upon the inheritance of Your Son. For the sake of His sorrowful Passion, grant them Your blessing and surround them with Your constant protection. Thus may they never fail in love or lose the treasure of the holy faith, but rather, with all the hosts of Angels and Saints, may they glorify Your boundless mercy for endless ages. Amen.
(Then pray the Chaplet to the Divine Mercy)

Fourth Day

Today bring to Me those who do not believe in God and those who do not yet know me. I was thinking also of them during My bitter Passion, and their future zeal comforted My Heart. Immerse them in the ocean of My mercy.

Most compassionate Jesus, You are the Light of the whole world. Receive into the abode of Your Most Compassionate Heart the souls of those who do not believe in God and of those who as yet do not know You. Let the rays of Your grace enlighten them that they, too, together with us, may extol Your wonderful mercy; and do not let them escape from the abode which is Your Most Compassionate Heart.

Eternal Father, turn Your merciful gaze upon the souls of those who do not believe in You, and of those who as yet do not know You, but who are enclosed in the Most Compassionate Heart of Jesus. Draw them to the light of the Gospel. These souls do not know what great happiness it is to love You. Grant that they, too, may extol the generosity of Your mercy for endless ages. Amen
(Then pray the Chaplet to the Divine Mercy)

Fifth Day

Today bring to Me the souls of those who have separated themselves from My Church, and immerse them in the ocean of My mercy. During My bitter Passion they tore at My Body and Heart, that is, My Church. As they return to unity with the Church, My wounds heal and in this way they alleviate My Passion.

Most Merciful Jesus, Goodness Itself, You do not refuse light to those who seek it of You. Receive into the abode of Your Most Compassionate Heart the souls of those who have separated themselves from Your Church. Draw them by Your light into the unity of the Church, and do not let them escape from the abode of Your Most Compassionate Heart; but bring it about that they, too, come to glorify the generosity of Your mercy.

Eternal Father, turn Your merciful gaze upon the souls of those who have separated themselves from Your Son's Church, who have squandered Your blessings and misused Your graces by obstinately persisting in their errors. Do not look upon their errors, but upon the love of Your own Son and upon His bitter Passion, which He underwent for their sake, since they, too, are enclosed in His Most Compassionate Heart. Bring it about that they also may glorify Your great mercy for endless ages. Amen.
(Then pray the Chaplet to the Divine Mercy)

Sixth Day

Today bring to Me the meek and humble souls and the souls of little children, and immerse them in My mercy. These souls most closely resemble My Heart. They strengthened Me during My bitter agony. I saw them as earthly Angels, who will keep vigil at My altars. I pour out upon them whole torrents of grace. Only the humble soul is capable of receiving My grace. I favour humble souls with My confidence.

Most Merciful Jesus, You yourself have said, "Learn from Me for I am meek and humble of heart." Receive into the abode of Your Most Compassionate Heart all meek and humble souls and the souls of little children. These souls send all heaven into ecstasy and they are the heavenly Father's favourites. They are a sweet-smelling bouquet before the throne of God; God Himself takes delight in their fragrance. These souls have a permanent abode in Your Most Compassionate Heart, O Jesus, and they unceasingly sing out a hymn of love and mercy.

Eternal Father, turn Your merciful gaze upon meek souls, upon humble souls, and upon little children who are enfolded in the abode which is the Most Compassionate Heart of Jesus. These souls bear the closest resemblance to Your Son. Their fragrance rises from the earth and reaches Your very throne. Father of mercy and of all goodness, I beg You by the love You bear these souls and by the delight You take in them: Bless the whole world, that all souls together may sing out the praises of Your mercy for endless ages. Amen.
(Then pray the Chaplet to the Divine Mercy)

Seventh Day

Today bring to Me the souls who especially venerate and glorify My mercy, and immerse them in My mercy. These souls sorrowed most over my Passion and entered most deeply into My spirit. They are living images of My Compassionate Heart. These souls will shine with a special brightness in the next life. Not one of them will go into the fire of hell. I shall particularly defend each one of them at the hour of death.

Most Merciful Jesus, whose Heart is Love Itself, receive into the abode of Your Most Compassionate Heart the souls of those who particularly extol and venerate the greatness of Your mercy. These souls are mighty with the very power of God Himself. In the midst of all afflictions and adversities they go forward, confident of Your mercy; and united to You, O Jesus, they carry all mankind on their shoulders. These souls will not be judged severely, but Your mercy will embrace them as they depart from this life.

Eternal Father, turn Your merciful gaze upon the souls who glorify and venerate Your greatest attribute, that of Your fathomless mercy, and who are enclosed in the Most Compassionate Heart of Jesus. These souls are a living Gospel; their hands are full of deeds of mercy, and their hearts, overflowing with joy, sing a canticle of mercy to You, O Most High! I beg You O God:

Show them Your mercy according to the hope and trust they have placed in You. Let there be accomplished in them the promise of Jesus, who said to them: I Myself will defend as My own glory, during their lifetime, and especially at the hour of their death, those souls who will venerate My fathomless mercy. Amen
(Then pray the Chaplet to the Divine Mercy)

Eighth Day

Today bring to Me the souls who are detained in purgatory, and immerse them in the abyss of My mercy. Let the torrents of My Blood cool down their scorching flames. All these souls are greatly loved by Me. They are

*making retribution to My justice. It is in your power to
bring them relief. Draw all the indulgences from the
treasury of My Church and offer them on their behalf. Oh,
if you only knew the torments they suffer, you would
continually offer for them the alms of the spirit and pay
off their debt to My justice.*

Most Merciful Jesus, You Yourself have said that You
desire mercy; so I bring into the abode of Your Most
Compassionate Heart the souls in Purgatory, souls who
are very dear to You, and yet, who must make retribution
to Your justice. May the streams of Blood and Water
which gushed forth from Your Heart put out the flames of
Purgatory, that there, too, the power of Your mercy may
be celebrated.

Eternal Father, turn Your merciful gaze upon the souls
suffering in Purgatory, who are enfolded in the Most
Compassionate Heart of Jesus. I beg You, by the
sorrowful Passion of Jesus Your Son, and by all the
bitterness with which His most sacred Soul was flooded:
Manifest Your mercy to the souls who are under Your just
scrutiny. Look upon them in no other way but only
through the Wounds of Jesus, Your dearly beloved Son;
for we firmly believe that there is no limit to Your
goodness and compassion. Amen.

(Then pray the Chaplet to the Divine Mercy)

Ninth Day

Today bring to Me souls who have become lukewarm, and immerse them in the abyss of My mercy. These souls wound My Heart most painfully. My soul suffered the most dreadful loathing in the Garden of Olives because of lukewarm souls. They were the reason I cried out: 'Father, take this cup away from Me, if it be Your will.' For them, the last hope of salvation is to flee to My mercy.

Most compassionate Jesus, You are Compassion Itself. I bring lukewarm souls into the abode of Your Most Compassionate Heart. In this fire of Your pure love, let these tepid souls, who, like corpses, filled You with such deep loathing, be once again set aflame. O Most Compassionate Jesus, exercise the omnipotence of Your mercy and draw them into the very ardour of Your love, and bestow upon them the gift of holy love, for nothing is beyond Your power.

Eternal Father, turn Your merciful gaze upon lukewarm souls who are nonetheless enfolded in the Most Compassionate Heart of Jesus. Father of Mercy, I beg You by the bitter Passion of Your Son and by His three-hour agony on the Cross: Let them, too, glorify the abyss of Your mercy. Amen.

(Then pray the Chaplet to the Divine Mercy)

THREE O'CLOCK PRAYERS

The choice of the three O'clock prayers depends on individual circumstances - you can follow Jesus' advice given to Sister Faustina:

> My daughter, try your best to make the Stations of the Cross in this hour, provided that your duties permit it; and if you are not able to make the Stations of the Cross, then at least step into the chapel for a moment and adore, in the Most Blessed Sacrament, My Heart, which is full of mercy; and should you be unable to step into the chapel, immerse yourself in prayer there where you happen to be, if only for a very brief instant. (1572)

Little prayers for use at the Hour of Great Mercy:

- You expired, Jesus, but the source of life gushed forth for souls, and the ocean of mercy opened up for the whole world. O Fount of Life, unfathomable Divine Mercy, envelop the whole world and empty Yourself out upon us. Amen. (1319)

- O Blood and Water, which gushed forth from the Heart of Jesus as a fount of mercy for us, I trust in You!(84) (*Repeat three times*)

- Divine Mercy Chaplet *(see page 60)*

Litany to the Divine Mercy

Lord, have mercy. Christ, have mercy. Lord, have mercy.
Christ, hear us. Christ, graciously hear us.
God, the Father of heaven, *have mercy on us (repeat)*.
God, the Son, Redeemer of the world.
God, the Holy Spirit.
Holy Trinity, one God.

Divine Mercy, greatest attribute of God,
   I trust in You (repeat).
Divine Mercy, unfathomable love of the Sanctifier.
Divine Mercy, incomprehensible mystery of the Most
   Blessed Trinity.
Divine Mercy, expression of the greatest might of God.
Divine Mercy, in creation of heavenly spirits.
Divine Mercy, in calling us forth from nothingness to
   existence.
Divine Mercy, encompassing the whole universe.
Divine Mercy, endowing us with immortal life.
Divine Mercy, shielding us from deserved punishment.
Divine Mercy, lifting us from the misery of sin.
Divine Mercy, justifying us through the Person of the
   Incarnate Word.
Divine Mercy, which flowed out from the wounds of Christ.
Divine Mercy, gushing forth from the Sacred Heart of Jesus.

Divine Mercy, giving us the Blessed Virgin Mary as Mother of Mercy.

Divine Mercy, in revealing the mysteries of God.

Divine Mercy, in the founding of the Holy Church.

Divine Mercy, in instituting the Holy Sacraments.

Divine Mercy, first of all in the sacraments of Baptism and Penance.

Divine Mercy, in the Holy Eucharist and the sacrament of Holy Orders.

Divine Mercy, in calling us to the holy faith.

Divine Mercy, in the conversion of sinners.

Divine Mercy, in sanctifying the just.

Divine Mercy, in perfecting of the pious.

Divine Mercy, fount of help for the sick and the suffering.

Divine Mercy, sweet relief for anguished hearts.

Divine Mercy, only hope of despairing souls.

Divine Mercy, accompanying us in every moment of our life.

Divine Mercy, anticipating our needs with graces.

Divine Mercy, repose of the dying.

Divine Mercy, heavenly delight of the saved.

Divine Mercy, respite and relief of the souls in Purgatory.

Divine Mercy, crown of All Saints.

Divine Mercy, inexhaustible source of miracles.

Lamb of God, who revealed the greatest mercy in redeeming the world by dying on the cross, *spare us, O Lord.*

Lamb of God, who mercifully offer Yourself for our sake in every holy Mass, *graciously hear us, O Lord.*

Lamb of God, who take away our sins with inexhaustible compassion, *have mercy on us.*

V: The Mercy of God is above all His works.

R: Hence, we will praise The Divine Mercy forever and ever.

Let us pray:

Eternal Father, in whom mercy is endless and the treasury of compassion inexhaustible, look kindly upon us and increase Your mercy in us, that in difficult moments we might not despair nor become despondent, but with great confidence submit ourselves to Your holy will, which is Love and Mercy itself (950). Through our Lord Jesus Christ, King of mercy, who with You and the Holy Spirit shows us mercy now and forever. R: Amen.

OTHER PRAYERS

Prayer to the Divine Mercy

O Greatly Merciful God, Infinite Goodness, today all mankind calls out from the abyss of its misery to Your mercy - to Your compassion, O God; and it is with its mighty voice of misery that it cries out.

Gracious God, do not reject the prayer of this earth's exiles! O Lord, Goodness beyond our understanding, Who are acquainted with our misery through and through, and know that by our own power we cannot ascend to You, we implore You; anticipate us with Your grace and keep on increasing Your mercy in us, that we may faithfully do Your holy will all through our life and at death's hour.

Let the omnipotence of Your mercy shield us from the darts of our salvation's enemies, that we may with confidence, as Your children, await Your final coming - that day known to You alone. And we expect to obtain everything promised us by Jesus in spite of all our wretchedness. For Jesus is our Hope: Through His merciful Heart as through an open gate we pass through to heaven. (1570)

Prayer to the Mother of Mercy

O Mary, my Mother and my Lady, I offer You my soul, my body, my life and my death and all that will follow it. I place everything in Your hands - O my Mother, cover my soul with Your virginal mantle and grant me the grace of purity of heart, soul and body. Defend me with Your power against all enemies, and especially against those who hide their malice behind the mask of virtue. (79) Fortify my soul, let pain not break it. Mother of grace, teach me to live by God's power. Amen.

O Mary, a terrible sword has pierced Your holy soul. Except for God, no one knows of Your suffering. Your soul does not break; it is brave, because it is with Jesus.

Sweet Mother, unite my soul to Jesus, because it is only then that I will be able to endure all trials and tribulations, and only in union with Jesus will my little sacrifices be pleasing to God. Sweetest Mother, continue to teach me about the interior life. May the sword of suffering never break me. O pure Virgin, pour courage into my heart and guard it. Amen. (915)

Prayer for acceptance of God's will

May You be blessed, O God, for everything You send me. Nothing under the sun happens without Your will. I cannot penetrate Your secrets with regard to myself, but I press my lips to the chalice You offer me. (1208)

O my God, I am ready to accept Your will in every detail, whatever it may be. However You may direct me, I will bless You. Whatever You ask of me I will do with the help of Your grace. Whatever Your holy will regarding me might be. I accept it with my whole heart and soul, taking no account of what my corrupt nature tells me. (1356)

Do what You will with me, O Jesus; I will adore You in everything. May Your will be done in me, O my Lord and my God, and I will praise Your infinite mercy. (78)

I am totally in accord with Your will; do with me as You please, O Lord, but only grant me the grace of loving You more and more ardently. This is what is most precious to me. I desire nothing but You, O Love Eternal!

It matters not along what paths You will lead me, paths of pain or paths of joy. I want to love You at every moment of my life. (751)

So today I submit myself completely and with loving consent to Your holy will, O Lord, and to Your most wise decrees, which are always full of clemency and mercy for me, though at times I can neither understand nor fathom them. O my Master. I surrender myself completely to You, who are the rudder of my soul; steer it Yourself according to Your divine wishes. I enclose myself in Your most compassionate Heart, which is a sea of unfathomable mercy. (1450)

Prayer for enlightenment

O Eternal and incomprehensible Love, I beg You for one grace: enlighten my mind with light from on high; help me to know and appreciate all things according to their value. I feel the greatest joy in my soul when I come to know the truth. (410)

Eternal Truth, give me a ray of Your light that I may come to know You, O Lord, and worthily glorify Your infinite mercy. And at the same time, grant me to know myself, the whole abyss of misery that I am. (727)

Jesus, give me an intellect, a great intellect, for this only, that I may understand You better; because the better I get to know You, the more ardently will I love You. Jesus, I ask You for a powerful intellect, that I may understand divine and lofty matters. Jesus, give me a keen intellect with which I will get to know Your Divine Essence and Your indwelling Triune life. Give my intellect these capacities and aptitudes by means of Your special grace. Although I know that there is a capability through grace which the Church gives me, there is still a treasure of graces which You give us, O Lord, when we ask You for them. But if my request is not pleasing to You, then I beg You, do not give me the inclination to pray thus. (1474)

Prayer for healing

Jesus, may Your pure and healthy blood circulate in my ailing organism, and may Your pure and healthy body transform my weak body, and may a healthy and vigorous life throb within me, if it is truly Your holy will that I should set about the work in question; and this will be a clear sign of Your holy will for me. (1089)

Prayer for trust

O my God, my only hope, I have placed all my trust in You, and I know I shall not be disappointed. (317)

I have understood that at certain and most difficult moments I shall be alone, deserted by everyone, and that I must face all the storms and fight with all the strength of my soul, even with those from whom I expected to get help. But I am not alone, because Jesus is with me, and with Him I fear nothing. I am well aware of everything, and I know what God is demanding of me. Suffering, contempt, ridicule, persecution and humiliation will be my constant lot. I know no other way. For sincere love ingratitude; this is my path, marked out by the footprints of Jesus. My Jesus, my strength and my only hope, in You alone is all my hope. My trust will not be frustrated. (746)

O Jesus, eternal Truth, strengthen my feeble forces; You can do all things, Lord. I know that without You all my efforts are in vain. O Jesus, do not hide from me, for I cannot live without You. Listen to the cry of my soul. Your mercy has not been exhausted, Lord, so have pity on my misery. Your mercy surpasses the understanding of all Angels and people put together; and so, although it seems to me that You do not hear me, I put my trust in the ocean of Your mercy, and I know that my hope will not be deceived. (69)

Prayer in times of suffering

O Living Host, support me in this exile, that I may be empowered to walk faithfully in the footsteps of the Saviour. I do not ask, Lord, that You take me down from the cross, but I implore You to give me the strength to remain steadfast upon it. I want to be stretched out upon the cross as You were, Jesus. I want all the tortures and pains that You suffered. I want to drink the cup of bitterness to the dregs. (1484)

O my Jesus, give me strength to endure suffering so that I may not make a wry face when I drink the cup of bitterness. Help me Yourself to make my sacrifice pleasing to You. May it not be tainted by my self-love... may everything that is in me, both my misery and my strength, give praise to You, O Lord. (1740)

Prayer for a happy death

O merciful Jesus, stretched on the cross, be mindful of the hour of our death. O most merciful Heart of Jesus, opened with a lance, shelter me at the last moment of my life. O Blood and Water, which gushed forth from the Heart of Jesus as a fount of unfathomable mercy for me [cleanse me of my sins and offences]. O dying Jesus, Hostage of mercy, avert the Divine wrath at the hour of my death. (813)

O my Jesus, may the last days of my exile be spent totally according to Your most holy will. I unite my sufferings, my bitterness and my last agony itself to Your Sacred Passion; and I offer myself for the whole world to implore an abundance of God's mercy for souls, and in particular for the souls [of sinners]. I firmly trust and commit myself entirely to Your holy will, which is mercy itself. Your mercy will be everything for me at the last hour. (1574)

Prayer for the grace to be merciful towards others

I want to be completely transformed into Your Mercy and to be Your living reflection, O Lord. May the greatest of all divine attributes, that of Your unfathomable mercy, pass through my heart and soul to my neighbour.

Help me, O Lord, that my eyes may be merciful, so that I may never suspect or judge from appearances, but look for what is beautiful in my neighbours' souls and come to their rescue.

Help me, that my ears may be merciful, so that I may give heed to my neighbours' needs and not be indifferent to their pains and moanings.

Help me, O Lord, that my tongue may be merciful, so that I should never speak negatively of my neighbour, but have a word of comfort and forgiveness for all.

Help me, O Lord, that my hands may be merciful and filled with good deeds, so that I may do only good to my neighbours and take upon myself the more difficult and toilsome tasks.

Help me, that my feet may be merciful, so that I may hurry to assist my neighbour, overcoming my own fatigue and weariness. My true rest is in the service of my neighbour.

Help me, O Lord, that my heart may be merciful so that I myself may feel all the sufferings of my neighbour. I will refuse my heart to no one, I will be sincere even with those who, I know, will abuse my kindness. And I will lock myself up in the most merciful Heart of Jesus. I will bear my own suffering in silence. May Your Mercy, O Lord, rest upon me. (163)

Prayer for sinners

You always console Me when you pray for sinners. The prayer most pleasing to Me is the prayer for the conversion of sinners. Know, My daughter, that this prayer is always heard and answered. (1397)

O Jesus, eternal Truth, our Life, I call upon You and I beg Your mercy for poor sinners. O sweetest Heart of my Lord, full of pity and unfathomable mercy, I plead with You for poor sinners. O Most Sacred Heart, Fount of Mercy from which gush forth rays of inconceivable graces upon the entire human race, I beg of You light for poor sinners. O Jesus, be mindful of Your own bitter Passion and do not permit the loss of souls redeemed at so dear a price of Your most precious Blood. O Jesus, when I consider the great price of Your Blood, I rejoice at its immensity, for one drop alone would have been enough for the salvation of all sinners. Although sin is an abyss of wickedness and ingratitude, the price paid for us can never be equalled. Therefore, let every soul trust in the Passion of the Lord and place its hope in His Mercy. God will not deny His mercy to anyone. Heaven and earth may change, but God's mercy will never be exhausted. Oh, what immense joy burns in my heart when I contemplate Your incomprehensible goodness, O Jesus! I desire to bring all sinners to Your feet that they may glorify Your mercy throughout endless ages. Amen. (72)

Prayer for the dying

Sr Faustina: When I entered my solitude, I heard these words:

At the hour of their death, I defend as My own glory every soul that will say this chaplet; or when others say it for a dying person, the pardon is the same. When this chaplet is said by the bedside of a dying person, God's anger is placated, unfathomable mercy envelops the soul, and the very depths of My tender mercy are moved for the sake of the sorrowful Passion of My Son. (811)

My daughter, encourage souls to say the chaplet which I have given to you. It pleases Me to grant everything they ask of Me by saying the chaplet. When hardened sinners say it, I will fill their souls with peace, and the hour of their death will be a happy one.

Write this for the benefit of distressed souls: when a soul sees and realises the gravity of its sins, when the whole abyss of the misery into which it immersed itself is displayed before its eyes, let it not despair, but with trust let it throw itself into the arms of My mercy, as a child into the arms of its beloved mother. These souls have a right of priority to My compassionate Heart, they have first access to My mercy. Tell them that no soul that has called upon My mercy has been disappointed or brought to shame. I delight particularly in a soul which has placed its trust in My goodness.

Write that when they say this chaplet in the presence of the dying, I will stand between My Father and the dying person, not as the just Judge but as the merciful Saviour. (1541)

My daughter, know that My Heart is mercy itself. From this sea of mercy, graces flow out upon the whole world. No soul that has approached Me has ever gone away unconsoled. All misery gets buried in the depths of My mercy, and every saving and sanctifying grace flows from this fountain. My daughter, I desire that your heart be an abiding place of My mercy. I desire that this mercy flow out upon the whole world through your heart. Let no one who approaches you go away without that trust in My mercy which I so ardently desire for souls.

Pray as much as you can for the dying. By your entreaties, obtain for them trust in My mercy, because they have most need of trust, and have it the least. Be assured that the grace of eternal salvation for certain souls in their final moment depends on your prayer. You know the whole abyss of My mercy, so draw upon it for yourself and especially for poor sinners. Sooner would heaven and earth turn into nothingness than would My mercy not embrace a trusting soul. (1777)

Prayer for the Holy Souls

Today bring to Me the souls who are in the prison of Purgatory, and immerse them in the abyss of My mercy. Let the torrents of My Blood cool down their scorching flames. All these souls are greatly loved by Me. They are making retribution to My justice. It is in your power to bring them relief. Draw all the indulgences from the treasury of My Church and offer them on their behalf. Oh, if you only knew the torments they suffer, you would continually offer for them the alms of the spirit and pay off their debt to My justice. (1226)

Most Merciful Jesus, You Yourself have said that You desire mercy; so I bring into the abode of Your Most Compassionate Heart the souls in Purgatory, souls who are very dear to You, and yet, who must make retribution to Your justice. May the streams of Blood and Water which gushed forth from Your Heart put out the flames of the purifying fire, that in that place, too, the power of Your mercy may be praised.

> From the terrible heat of the cleansing fire
> Rises a plaint to Your mercy,
> And they receive comfort, refreshment, relief
> In the stream of mingled Blood and Water.

Eternal Father, turn Your merciful gaze upon the souls suffering in Purgatory, who are enfolded in the Most Compassionate Heart of Jesus. I beg You, by the sorrowful Passion of Jesus Your Son, and by all the bitterness with which His most sacred Soul was flooded, manifest Your mercy to the souls who are under Your just scrutiny. Look upon them in no other way than through the Wounds of Jesus, Your dearly beloved Son; for we firmly believe that there is no limit to Your goodness and compassion. (1227)

Prayer for priests

O my Jesus, I beg You on behalf of the whole Church; Grant it love and the light of Your Spirit, and give power to the words of priests so that hardened hearts might be brought to repentance and return to You, O Lord. Lord, give us holy priests; You yourself maintain them in holiness. O Divine and Great High Priest, may the power of Your mercy accompany them everywhere and protect them from the devil's traps and snares which are continually being set for the souls of priests. May the power of Your mercy, O Lord, shatter and bring to naught all that might tarnish the sanctity of priests, for You can do all things. (1052)

The Lord said to me, My daughter, do not tire of proclaiming My mercy. In this way you will refresh this Heart of Mine, which burns with a flame of pity for sinners.

Tell My priests that hardened sinners will repent on hearing their words when they speak about My unfathomable mercy, about the compassion I have for them in My Heart. To priests who proclaim and extol My mercy, I will give wondrous power; I will anoint their words and touch the hearts of those to whom they will speak. (1521)

Prayer for one's native country

Most Merciful Jesus, I beseech You through the intercession of Your Saints, and especially the intercession of Your dearest Mother who nurtured You from childhood, bless my native land. I beg You, Jesus, look not on our sins, but on the tears of little children, on the hunger and cold they suffer. Jesus, for the sake of these innocent ones, grant me the grace that I am asking of You for my country. (286)

Short, exclamatory prayers

Most Merciful Heart of Jesus, protect us from the just anger of God. (1526)

O Christ, although much effort is required, all things can be done with Your grace. (1696)

O my Jesus, I am making at this very moment a firm and eternal resolution by virtue of Your grace and mercy, fidelity to the tiniest grace of Yours. (716)

With Jesus, through Jesus and in Jesus is my communion with You, Eternal Father. (648)

O my God, I love You. (1323)

King of Mercy, guide my soul. (3)

Jesus, I trust in You; I trust in the ocean of Your mercy. You are a Mother to me. (249)

O my God, my only hope, I have placed all my trust in You, and I know I shall not be disappointed. (317)

O purest love, rule in all Your plenitude in my heart and help me to do Your holy will most faithfully! (328)

Jesus, Life and Truth, my Master, guide every step of my life, that I may act according to Your holy will. (688)

My Jesus, my strength and my only hope, in You alone is all my hope. My trust will not be frustrated. (746)

O Jesus, have mercy! Embrace the whole world and press me to Your Heart... O Lord, let my soul repose in the sea of Your unfathomable mercy. (869)

Hide me, Jesus, in the depths of Your mercy, and then let my neighbour judge me as he pleases. (791)

O Jesus, shield me with Your mercy and also judge me leniently, or else Your justice may rightly damn me. (1093)

Prayers through the Intercession of St Faustina

Litany to St Faustina

Lord, have mercy. Christ, have mercy. Lord, have mercy.

Christ, hear us. Christ, graciously hear us.

God the Father of heaven, *have mercy on us (repeat)*.

God the Son, Redeemer of the world.

God the Holy Spirit.

Holy Trinity, one God.

Holy Mary, *pray for us (repeat)*.

Saint Faustina, living witness of the heavenly Father's mercy.

Saint Faustina, humble servant of Jesus, Mercy Incarnate.

Saint Faustina, obedient instrument of the Spirit, the Comforter.

Saint Faustina, trustful daughter of the Mother of Mercy.

Saint Faustina, confidante of the Divine Mercy message.

Saint Faustina, faithful secretary of the words of the Merciful Jesus.

Saint Faustina, great apostle of God's mercy.

Saint Faustina, dispenser of God, rich in mercy.

Saint Faustina, gift of God for the whole world.

Saint Faustina, perceiving the goodness of the Creator in every creature.

Saint Faustina, glorifying God in the mystery of the Incarnation.

Saint Faustina, partaker in the Lord's passion and resurrection.

Saint Faustina, guide on the way of Jesus' cross.

Saint Faustina, meeting with Jesus in the holy sacraments.

Saint Faustina, united with the Spouse in your soul.

Saint Faustina, enraptured by the mercy of God in Mary's life.

Saint Faustina, loving the Church, the Mystical Body of Christ.

Saint Faustina, powerful with genuine faith.

Saint Faustina, persevering in unwavering hope.

Saint Faustina, enkindled with ardent love.

Saint Faustina, beautiful with true humility.

Saint Faustina, simple with childlike trust.

Saint Faustina, model of fulfilling God's will.

Saint Faustina, example of generous service.

Saint Faustina, caring protector of the souls of priests and religious.

Saint Faustina, defender of young people and children against evil.

Saint Faustina, hope of the fallen and the despairing.

Saint Faustina, strength of the sick and the suffering.

Saint Faustina, safeguarding trust in the hearts of the dying.

Saint Faustina, offering yourself for sinners.

Saint Faustina, solicitous for the salvation of all people.

Saint Faustina, advocate of the suffering souls in purgatory.

Saint Faustina, imploring God's mercy for the whole world.

Lamb of God, who take away the sins of the world, *spare us, O Lord.*

Lamb of God, who take away the sins of the world, *graciously hear us, O Lord.*

Lamb of God, who take away the sins of the world, *have mercy on us.*

V: Pray for us, Saint Faustina.

R: That we may proclaim the message of Mercy to the world with our life and words.

Let us pray:

Merciful God, receive our thanksgiving for the gift of Saint Faustina's life and mission. Grant, we beseech You, that by her intercession we may grow in the attitude of trust in You and mercy toward our neighbour. Through Christ, our Lord. Amen.

NOVENA TO ST FAUSTINA

First Day

The Knowledge of the Mystery of Divine Mercy

Jesus: Your life is to be modelled on Mine, from the crib to My death on the Cross. Penetrate My mysteries, and you will know the abyss of My mercy towards creatures and My unfathomable goodness - and this you shall make known to the world. (438)

Sr Faustina: O God, how I desire that souls come to know You and to see that You have created them because of Your unfathomable love; O my Creator and Lord I feel that I am going to remove the veil of heaven so that earth will not doubt Your goodness. (483)

Saint Faustina, obtain for me the grace of penetrating more and more deeply into the mystery of God's mercy in the work of creation, salvation and glory so that, like you, I may make it known to the world.
Our Father, Hail Mary, Glory Be.

Second Day

The Contemplation of Mercy in Everyday Life

Jesus: When you reflect upon what I tell you in the depths of your heart, you profit more than if you had read many books. Oh, if souls would only want to listen to My voice when I am speaking in the depths of their hearts, they would reach the peak of holiness in a short time. (584)

Sr Faustina: God I look for no happiness beyond my own interior where You dwell. I rejoice that You dwell within me; here I abide with You unendingly; it is here that my greatest intimacy with You exists; here I dwell with You in safety; here is a place not probed by the human eye. The Blessed Virgin encourages me to commune with You in this way. (cf. 454)

Saint Faustina, teach me to abide with the Lord in my own soul, to listen to His voice and to experience with Him all the moments of my life. Obtain for me the grace of contemplating mercy in everyday life.
Our Father, Hail Mary, Glory Be.

Third Day

The Attitude of Trust toward God

Jesus: My daughter, if I demand through you that people revere My mercy, you should be the first to distinguish yourself by this confidence in My mercy (742). I assure you of a permanent income on which you will live. Your duty will be to trust completely in My goodness, and My duty will be to give you all you need. I am making Myself dependent upon your trust: if your trust is great, then My generosity will be without limit. (548)

Sr Faustina: God, One in the Holy Trinity, I want to love You as no human soul has ever loved You before; and although I am utterly miserable and small, I have, nevertheless, cast the anchor of my trust deep down into the abyss of Your mercy, O my God and Creator! In spite of my great misery I fear nothing, but hope to sing You a hymn of glory for ever. (283)

Saint Faustina, obtain for me the grace of childlike trust so that I may always and in everything faithfully fulfil God's will, which is mercy itself for us.

Our Father, Hail Mary, Glory Be.

Fourth Day

The Attitude of Mercy toward Neighbour

Jesus: My daughter,... I demand from you deeds of mercy, which are to arise out of love for Me. You are to show mercy to your neighbours always and everywhere. You must not shrink from this or try to excuse or absolve yourself from it. I am giving you three ways of exercising mercy toward your neighbour: the first - by deed, the second - by word, the third - by prayer. In these three degrees is contained the fullness of mercy, and it is an unquestionable proof of love for Me. By this means a soul glorifies and pays reverence to My mercy. (742)

Sr Faustina: My Jesus, penetrate me through and through so that I might be able to reflect You in my whole life. Divinize me so that my deeds may have supernatural value. Grant that I may have love, compassion and mercy for every soul without exception. O my Jesus, each of Your saints reflects one of Your virtues; I desire to reflect Your compassionate heart, full of mercy; I want to glorify it. Let Your mercy, O Jesus, be impressed upon my heart and soul like a seal, and this will be my badge in this and the future life. (1242)

Saint Faustina, intercede for me before the Lord so that my life, too, may be transformed into mercy exercised toward my neighbour by deed, word and prayer. May my eyes, ears, mouth, hands, feet, and heart be merciful.
Our Father, Hail Mary, Glory Be.

Fifth Day

Proclaiming the Message of Mercy

Jesus: In the Old Covenant I sent prophets wielding thunderbolts to My people. Today I am sending you with My mercy to the people of the whole world. I do not want to punish aching mankind, but I desire to heal it, pressing it to My Merciful Heart. I use punishment when they themselves force Me to do so; My hand is reluctant to take hold of the sword of justice. Before The Day of Justice I am sending The Day of Mercy. (1588)

Sr Faustina: O my God, let everything that is in me praise You, my Lord and Creator; and with every beat of my heart I want to praise Your unfathomable mercy. I want to tell souls of Your goodness and encourage them to trust in Your mercy. That is my mission, which You Yourself have entrusted to me, O Lord, in this life and in the life to come. (1325)

Following your example, Saint Faustina, I want to proclaim to the world the message of Mercy by the witness of my life and word so that it may reach all the peoples of the earth and fill their hearts with hope. May Jesus' promise be fulfilled in my life as well: Souls who spread the honour of My mercy I shield through their entire lives as a tender mother her infant, and at the hour of death I will not be a Judge for them, but the Merciful Saviour. (1075) *Our Father, Hail Mary, Glory Be.*

Sixth Day

Imploring God's Mercy for the World

Jesus: My daughter, I have inclined My heart to your requests. Your assignment and duty here on earth is to beg for mercy for the whole world (570). You will join prayers, fasts, mortifications, labours and all sufferings to My prayer, fasting, mortification, labours and sufferings and then they will have power before My Father (531). I am making you the administrator of My mercy (570).

Sr Faustina: O my God, I am conscious of my mission in the Holy Church. It is my constant endeavour to plead for mercy for the world. I unite myself closely with Jesus and stand before Him as an atoning sacrifice on behalf of the world. God will refuse me nothing when I entreat Him with the voice of His Son. My sacrifice is nothing in itself, but when I join it to the sacrifice of Jesus Christ, it becomes all-powerful and has the power to appease divine wrath. God loves us in His Son; the painful Passion of the Son of God constantly turns aside the wrath of God. (482)

Together with you, Saint Faustina, I want to plead for mercy for the whole world, particularly for sinners as well as for priests and religious so that, living in the world, they may lead the people of God on the paths of salvation. *Our Father, Hail Mary, Glory Be.*

Seventh Day

Love for the Church - The Mystical Body of Christ

Jesus: My daughter, consider the life of God which is found in the Church for the salvation and the sanctification of your soul. Consider the use that you make of these treasures of grace, of these efforts of My love. (1758)

Sr Faustina: Jesus, I am striving for sanctity, because in this way I shall be useful to the Church. I make constant efforts in practicing virtue. I try faithfully to follow Jesus. And I deposit this whole series of daily virtues - silent, hidden, almost imperceptible, but made with great love - in the treasury of God's Church for the common benefit of souls. I feel interiorly as if I were responsible for all souls. I know very well that I do not live for myself alone, but for the entire Church. (1505)

Grateful for all the gifts of God's mercy available to me in the Church, I want to make use of them like you, Saint Faustina, in order to become a saint and so draw other souls to the founts of God's mercy.
Our Father, Hail Mary, Glory Be.

Eighth Day

Meeting with Jesus in the Sacraments

Jesus: Oh, how painful it is to Me that souls so seldom unite themselves to Me in Holy Communion. I wait for souls, and they are indifferent toward Me. I love them tenderly and sincerely, and they distrust Me. I want to lavish My graces on them, and they do not want accept them. They treat Me as a dead object, whereas My Heart is full of love and mercy. In order that you may know at least some of My pain, imagine the most tender of mothers who has great love for her children, while those children spurn her love. Consider her pain. No one is in a position to console her. This is but a feeble image and likeness of My love. (1447)

Sr Faustina: Jesus, there is one more secret in my life, the deepest and dearest to my heart: it is You Yourself when You come to my heart under the appearance of bread. Herein lays the whole secret of my sanctity. Here my heart is so united with Yours as to be but one. There are no more secrets, because all that is Yours is mine, and all that is mine is Yours. Such is the omnipotence and the miracle of Your mercy. (1489) All the good that is in me is due to Holy Communion. I owe everything to it. I feel that this holy fire has transformed me completely. Oh, how happy I am to be a dwelling place for You, O Lord! My heart is a temple in which You dwell continually. (1392)

Saint Faustina, obtain for me the grace of living faith so that each sacrament be for me a privileged place of meeting with the Lord, and may the Eucharist be at the very centre of my entire life, transforming it into love.
Our Father, Hail Mary, Glory Be.

Ninth Day

Devotion to Our Lady

Mary: Your lives must be like Mine: quiet and hidden, in unceasing union with God, pleading for humanity and preparing the world for the second coming of God. (625)

Sr Faustina: O sweet Mother of God, I model my life on You. You are for me the bright dawn; in You I lose myself, enraptured. O Mother, Immaculate Virgin, in You the divine ray is reflected. Midst storms, 'tis You who teach me to love the Lord, O my shield and defence from the foe. (1232)

Saint Faustina, most faithful daughter of the Mother of Mercy, hide me under Her mantle so that She may lead me

to Jesus and teach me to participate in His life and mission of revealing to the world the mercy of the heavenly Father. Like Mary, I want to give Jesus - Mercy Incarnate - to people and prepare the world for His second coming.
Our Father, Hail Mary, Glory Be.

Prayer to obtain Graces
through the intercession of St Faustina

O Jesus, who filled Saint Faustina with profound veneration for Your boundless Mercy, deign, if it be Your holy will, to grant me, through her intercession, the grace for which I fervently pray... My sins render me unworthy of Your Mercy, but be mindful of Sister Faustina's spirit of sacrifice and self-denial, and reward her virtue by granting the petition which, with childlike trust, I present to You through her intercession.
Our Father, Hail Mary, Glory Be.

Saint Faustina, pray for us.

Act of Entrustment of the World to Divine Mercy

(Words of the Holy Father, John Paul II addressed at the shrine of Divine Mercy in Kraków, Łagiewniki, 17th August 2002)

God, merciful Father, in Your Son, Jesus Christ, You have revealed Your love and poured it out upon us in the Holy Spirit, the Comforter. We entrust to You today the destiny of the world and of every man and woman. Bend down to us sinners, heal our weakness, conquer all evil, and grant that all the peoples of the earth may experience Your mercy. In You, the Triune God, may they ever find the source of hope.

Eternal Father, by the Passion and Resurrection of Your Son, have mercy on us and upon the whole world! Amen.

St Sister Faustina